Once Upon a Tooth

. . . a Fairy's Tale

by Vickie Adair
Illustrated by Charlene Bostick

3rdc

A Third Coast Publishers LLP Publication

Once Upon a Tooth...
  a Fairy's Tale

First Edition

Text & Illustrations © 2010
by Vickie Adair & Charlene Bostick

Cover design & book layout by Third Coast Publishers LLP.

Published by Third Coast Publishers LLP.

For more information and other publications visit:
www.ThirdCoastPublishers.com

ISBN 978-0-9829498-0-1

Library of Congress Control Number: 2010935158

To my children who showed me the magic...

-Vickie

Eeling, a brave and curious little fairy, crept close to the human village. She went near enough to see and hear, but stayed hidden behind the leaves of a morning glory vine.

The other fairies had begged her to stay away from the feared humans, but she had been too curious to listen.

She looked at the houses humans had built. Why did they build them? All fairies find shelter among the plants in the beautiful forest.

Eeling watched the women making cloth and sewing clothes. Did they not know that soft green leaves made fine garments?

She watched the men making furniture, even though any stump or toadstool was fine to sit upon. Making carts was the one thing Eeling understood, because humans had no wings to carry them when they grew tired of walking.

Eeling sat in her morning glory vine for many days, watching the humans, trying to understand what she saw. She often heard bits and pieces of a whistled tune, laughter, or the distant sound of humming as they worked. Because she realized that human's strange ways made them happy, Eeling grew more curious.

She gathered her courage once again and, in the dark of night, flew down from her vine and crept into the village for a closer look.

When she drew near the first cottage, she noticed light streaming out of a window. She fluttered up and perched on the window ledge to peer inside. In the warm, cozy glow of a large fireplace, a pair of gray and wrinkled humans sat near each other.

No fairy ever became gray and wrinkled, so she watched the couple for a long time trying to understand the peaceful happiness of the scene. Then she decided this kind of happiness was something a fairy could never know. She turned away, leapt down from the ledge, and started towards the next cottage in hopes of finding a happiness she might understand and possibly share.

Through a window of the next cottage, Eeling looked into a room. In the glow of a single candle sat a young mother singing a lull-a-bye to her child. Eeling pressed close to the window glass so that she could hear.

Because fairies are never babies, just as they are never gray and wrinkled, no fairy had ever felt the warmth of a mother's love. But Eeling now felt that strange warmth inside her and felt that she might have missed something beautiful.

Wanting more of this strange warmth, she stayed as near as possible, watching the mother and child until the mother laid the sleeping child in its crib and left the room.

Eeling then felt what no fairy had ever felt before. She felt lonely.

Confused and tired, Eeling flew to a big tree near the cottage to rest. Finding the largest leaf, she sadly lay upon it and went to sleep. That night, for the first time, a fairy slept inside a village of humans.

The next morning Eeling woke with the sun shining in her face. She yawned, stretched, and fluttered her wings. Looking around the village, she saw that men and women were already up and very busy. She decided that she wanted to talk to the humans. From the shelter of the tree, she looked for the best human to approach.

Soon she saw a huge man, whose hair and beard were the color of fire, coming up the lane in her direction. He led a horse that nudged him gently on the shoulder, and a big yellow dog strutted closely at his heels.

When the human came closer, Eeling could see that his clothes were tattered and his large hands were rough. But, kindness and laughter sparkled in his eyes. This man was the human she felt she could trust, so off the leaf she flew, straight toward the human.

She stopped and fluttered her wings a few inches away from his face as he walked along. Eeling made her voice sound very brave.

"I am called Eeling, and I would like to know about humans."

The human raised his hand and waved it in front of his face as if some insect were buzzing around annoying him. He almost knocked Eeling from the air. She was very confused by this, but stayed near and tried again.

"I am called Eeling, and I would like to know about humans."

Again the human raised his hand and waved it around so that Eeling had to dart out of the way.

When Eeling realized that the human could not see her, she also knew that he heard her voice only as sounds, not as words. She did not understand his failure to see or understand her.

Was she invisible? Were her words nonsense?

To find out she flew up to the horse, and the horse saw her. He neighed, "Hello."

She flew over to the dog, who barked a "Hi" and then wagged his tail. Eeling curtsied back.

She was bewildered and wondered if all humans could not see or understand her. So, all that day, Eeling went from one person to another to find out.

She went to a human plowing in a field, a human weaving cloth, a human cutting a tree, and a human sowing seeds, but none of them saw her. And, unlike the big man with hair like fire, none of the others even heard a sound when she spoke!

By the time the sun began to go down, Eeling was very discouraged. Suddenly, she remembered that the night before, when she had listened to the mother singing to her child, she had felt happy. Eeling flew back to the same window.

This time the window was open, and she flew into the room. Eeling went to hover over the tiny human to take a closer look. The baby looked straight at her, then, made a gurgling sound that sounded like laughter. As none of the others humans had, the baby saw her!

Eeling looked closer into the child's eyes and saw magic, the same magic that the fairies found in the wild meadow flowers, the forest trees, and the earth itself.

She didn't understand why the baby had the magic and the grown humans did not, but now knew why the grown ones could not see her.

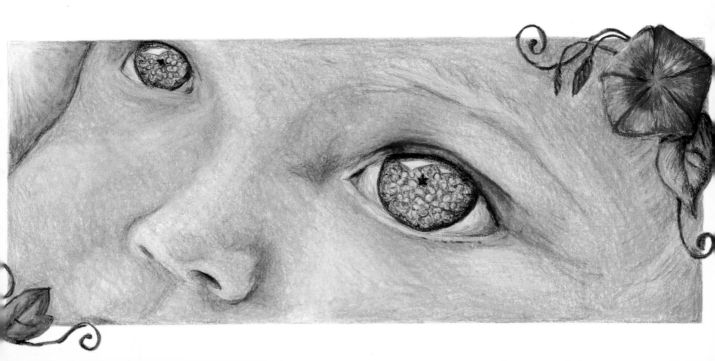

The young mother came into the room, picked up her baby, and settled down in the rocking chair. Eeling hurried over and perched on the arm of the rocker so that she could be rocked also.

The baby made its gurgling sound again when she saw Eeling sitting on the rocker. They spent a very pleasant evening together listening to the mother sing and speak softly.

As the night grew darker, the baby fell asleep in her mother's arms. The mother rose and laid the child gently in her crib. As Eeling watched, the mother kissed the baby lightly and murmured, "Sleep well, my Susie." Then she blew out the candle and left the room.

That night Eeling did not go to the big tree to sleep, but flew to the head of the crib and settled down there. She felt a need to watch over the child through the night to be sure the child stayed safe.

As she watched the sleeping child, a wonderful new feeling came to life in the heart of this single fairy, for Eeling was the first fairy to ever know love.

When the birds began to sing in the dawn, the mother came and carried Susie to another room in the cottage. Eeling knew that the child would be safe with her mother, so she stretched, flexed her wings, and flew out the window.

She felt a peaceful tiredness and knew that her night long watch had been work, a thing fairies never did. But, the work had given her a very nice and happy feeling.

She went to a nearby honeysuckle vine to eat some nectar, and then curled up inside the vine and slept. She slept soundly until mid-afternoon and woke up with a mission.

All through the rest of the afternoon, Eeling searched for the children of the village. All the very young children could see her! Eeling had great fun that day playing with the village children.

She let the children chase her as she darted around, just out of reach of their hands. She also hid in the leaves and let them find her.

A brown-haired boy had almost found her when he picked up a shiny coin and called to the others. All the children gathered excitedly around him wanting to see the coin. Eeling wondered why they were so excited.

As it began to get dark, she returned to Susie's cottage. Eeling knew that she need be in no hurry to return to the deep forest because time means little in the long life of a fairy. So, she stayed near the village, always going at night to hear the lull-a-byes and watch over Susie as she slept.

After she had rested each morning, Eeling would sometimes play with the children or go play by herself outside the village near the edge of the forest.

One day when she went to play alone, Eeling found a coin that some human had lost. It was pretty, and she knew the children liked the coins, so she hid it in the hollow of an old oak tree,

She had no use for coins as humans seemed to have. But because they were important to the children, from then on, she put all the coins she found in the oak tree.

As the years passed, Susie grew into a golden-haired little girl, who could run and play out-of-doors with Eeling. They talked often, and Eeling tried to teach this child she loved all the magic lore of the fairies.

These were the best days Eeling had ever had in her more than one hundred years because she had her special child to watch over, teach, and love.

During the fifth year that Eeling had lived near the village, a tooth fell out of Susie's mouth as they were playing chase. Alarmed, Eeling flew to Susie and asked if she was hurting.

As Eeling hovered near, Susie seemed confused and unable to hear or see Eeling clearly.

In great sadness, Eeling realized that Susie had lost a part of her magic, and she picked up the tooth and flew away with it to the hollow of the big oak tree where she kept her coins.

She supposed that she should not have taken Susie's tooth away with her, but she wished very much to keep this magical part of her child.

That night when Eeling left the tree to go and listen to the stories that Susie's mother now told at night, she carried one of her coins to replace the tooth that she had kept.

Susie could not see Eeling well during the story time that night, but she did seem to know that Eeling was nearby.

That night, Eeling watched over Susie as always, but before she left the next morning, she slipped the coin under Susie's pillow and gave her a very light fairy kiss.

Over the next three years, Susie continued to lose her magical teeth, and became less aware of Eeling's presence with the loss of each tooth. Finally, one bright summer day, Susie lost the last of her magic teeth.

Eeling rushed to her and flew around her face and tugged on her hair. She could tell that Susie could neither see nor hear her now. Sadly, she realized that Susie no longer even remembered a fairy called Eeling who loved her.

Eeling went to the hollow of the big oak tree and cried the first fairy tear that was ever shed.

She knew that her years with Susie had come to an end, but she wished to keep a part of Susie with her always.

She took all of Susie's magic teeth and, holding them in her hands, she used her magic and turned them into a fine sparkling dust.

Eeling put the dust in a pouch made of soft leaves and fine vines. She tied the pouch around her waist so that she might carry a part of Susie with her always.

She knew that she no longer needed to stay. So, the next morning, with a heavy-heart, Eeling started on her way back to the other fairies in the deep forest.

Suddenly, she stopped with a feeling that something was very wrong. Then the wind whispered to her that Susie needed her.

Eeling flew as fast as she could into the village. When she found Susie, there were tears rolling down the young girl's face, and she looked as if she didn't think life was much fun anymore.

Susie had lots of chores to do and was worried about starting school and being away from home.

Eeling could see that Susie was wishing she was a baby again with nothing to do but play. She wanted to help Susie, but what could she do since Susie no longer could see or hear her?

She couldn't do tricks in the air or make silly faces to make Susie laugh as she had when Susie still had her magic.

Then, she remembered the dust in her pouch. She didn't know what good it would do, but she reached into her pouch, took out just a pinch of the dust, and sprinkled it over Susie.

A totally new kind of magic flowed into Susie then. Her eyes began to sparkle. A smile lifted the corners of her mouth, and she sang a little song as she left to do the chores that needed to be done.

Eeling realized that because of the dust, Susie now saw that her life ahead could be as adventurous and as happy as she chose to make it.

With a happy heart Eeling set out once more for the deep forest, skipping and dancing along the way. She would keep Susie's magic safe for her.

Eeling knew that no matter how far apart they were, if Susie ever had need of her own magic dust, she would always know.

All through Susie's life, Eeling would be able to help her when she had need of a little magic, and that was all it took to make Eeling happy.

After Eeling returned to the fairy village, she was asked to tell her story of the little human child over and over. All the fairies were filled with wonder at the magic called love. Many of the fairies began to seek out their own human babies to love and watch over.

Now, whenever a new child is born, a fairy comes to love and protect the child's magical dust forever.

As for Eeling, she later became queen of all the fairies.

She lives still – deep in the magical forest.

Vickie:

My grandmother taught me to read when I was two, and it was always the stories that enthralled me, never the lessons. In elementary school, I was the playground storyteller often telling stories for the expressed purpose of frightening the other kids.

Over the course of years, I've used my Master's Degree in English for many paying jobs that did not include storytelling, but my heart is always in the weaving of a tale.

Charlene:

I remember hot summer afternoons sitting in front of the book shelf reading through encyclopedias, fairy tales, poetry, mythology, and a set of Childcraft books. Though I loved the stories, it was the art that moved me.

When I finally decided, at about fifty, it was time to figure out what I wanted to do when I grew up, I knew-- use that Design Degree from LSU to begin my career as an artist.